7 Qualities of a Man of Faith

by John Osteen

Unless otherwise indicated, all Scripture quotations in this book are from the King James Version of the Bible.

ISBN 0-912631-42-2

Lakewood Church
P.O. Box 23297
Houston, TX 77228

7 Qualities of a Man of Faith

Are you facing a struggle today? Is there something you need to believe God for? Do you feel surrounded by trouble on every side?

The Bible says, *All that will live godly in Christ Jesus shall suffer persecution* (2 Timothy 3:12). The time will come, if it hasn't already, when you're going to have to believe God for something—for your marriage, your finances, your children, your spiritual growth, your health. And you need to know how to come to Him in faith, how to stand on the word of faith.

The word of faith I live by today I learned in the midst of a great struggle in my life. It was either learn it or die...learn it or lose my health. And I learned it. The devil has attacked me since then, but he can't take me down. Now when fear knocks at my door, faith answers. I know how to stand.

So what makes the difference between living a life of victory or living one of defeat? What are the qualities of a man or woman of real faith? I believe they are exemplified by the life of one of the great men of faith in the Bible, Elijah.

Elijah was a great man of faith

James 5:17,18 says, *Elias was a man subject to like passions as we are, and he prayed earnestly that it might not rain: and it rained not on the earth by the space of three years and six months. And he prayed again, and the heaven gave rain, and the earth brought forth her fruit.*

Elias (or Elijah as he was called in the Old Testament) was a person just like you and me. Yet, he was a man of great faith. The Bible says he was subject to like passions as we are. *Passions* means "sufferings." So Elijah was a man subject to sufferings just as we are. In other words, he was just an ordinary man.

I once visited the Vatican in Rome, Italy. There are paintings and statues of the 12 apostles on the walls and in the halls, and they're all bigger than life. In fact, some of them are huge. That's the way we tend to think of the apostles. But the apostles weren't bigger than life—they were flesh and blood just like you and me. They were ordinary human beings. Somehow, because they're in the Bible, we think they were special—that they weren't like us. But that's not true.

Elijah was an ordinary man who had such great faith that when he prayed that it wouldn't rain, it didn't...for three and a half years.

You say, "Brother Osteen, how can a person have enough faith to stop the rain? I just don't have that much faith."

The Bible says, *Without faith it is impossible to please* [God]: *for he that cometh to God must believe that he is, and that he is a rewarder of them that diligently seek him* (Hebrews 11:6).

Without faith in God, it's impossible to be born again or to go to heaven. Ephesians 2:8,9 says, *For by grace are ye saved through faith; and that not of yourselves: it is the gift of God: not of works, lest any man should boast.*

God wants everyone to be saved, so He has given each of us the measure of faith. Paul wrote, *For I say, through the grace given unto me, to every man that is among you, not to think of himself more highly than he ought to think; but to think soberly, according as God hath dealt to every man **the measure of faith***

(Romans 12:3).

We all have the saving measure of faith. Everybody starts out with the same measure, the same size faith—just enough to get him saved. But the Bible says, *Your faith is growing more and more* (2 Thessalonians 1:3, NIV). That means our faith can grow.

We cannot grow in righteousness. Once we accept Christ, we become the righteousness of God (see 2 Corinthians 5:21), and we can never be more righteous than that. But we can grow in faith.

How does faith grow?

The more you use your arms and legs, the stronger they get. The more you walk and jog and exercise, the stronger and more fit your muscles become. But if you don't use a muscle, you'll lose it.

That's the way faith is. Faith will grow as you use it. The more you use it, the stronger it grows. But this growth is a gradual process.

You aren't disappointed in a baby because it can't stand up and run a marathon. You don't expect a baby to do that. You expect the child to grow and become stronger. You expect it to start crawling first, then pulling itself up and holding onto things, and finally taking a step or two. Eventually you know that child will be able to walk and run.

That's the way your faith is. It grows gradually as you use it. Many people make the mistake of trying to jump up and run in their faith life when they are just babies learning to crawl. They want big cars and mansions, and they say, "Well, if two of us agree that we want a mansion by three o'clock this afternoon and an expensive car by Saturday, then we'll get it." But when they don't get the mansion and the car, they lose faith. They say, "Well, this faith business just doesn't work!"

Of course it doesn't work—not like that! You need to stay in the realm where your faith is and not get beyond it.

I asked a man one time, "What do you do?" He said, "I don't work. I just live by faith." Well, he was deep in debt. That kind of behavior isn't faith; it's ignorance. The Bible says if a man doesn't work, he shouldn't eat (see 2 Thessalonians 3:10).

Don't be a flakey, off-the-wall, out-in-left-field individual and call yourself a faith person. If you are a faith person, you ought to have your needs supplied and have a good report. And the only way you can do that is to live according to your faith and allow your faith to grow.

I remember when my congregation and I began to believe God for our new building. In 1970 when I first returned to Lakewood Church, my faith was not developed. I had been having great evangelistic meetings across the country, and things had gone well. But my faith had not been truly challenged. I had not really exercised it, and my faith wasn't very strong in the beginning.

The first thing God showed me was to get a group of men from the church and challenge them. He showed me what each one of them was able to do and how to challenge each man to have faith to do what he could toward building a new building. (At the time we were meeting in an old tin barn.) We did it. We stretched our faith muscles. We developed a little bit...then a little bit more. Today we are in a beautiful church building seating 8,200. But we started small and worked toward the big.

You need to develop your faith gradually as you go along. Use your faith. Stretch your faith, or it will never grow.

Faith is believing the Word of God

Now, faith is simply believing God will do what He said. It's believing the Word of God. The New Testament uses two Greek words for the Word of God. One is *logos*, which is the revealed will of God, the plan of salvation, the context of the Bible. The other is *rhema*, which is a word God speaks to you. Suddenly a scripture comes alive as if God himself spoke it to you.

Faith not only comes from the *logos*, faith comes by hearing, and hearing by the *rhema* of God (see Romans 10:17). Once God speaks a scripture to you, believing it is easy because with that *rhema* comes faith.

I remember times God has quickened scriptures to me. It was just like He was reading my mail. He made a promise in His Word, I read that promise, and then He quickened that promise to me. I knew the promise would come true because I had the *logos* and the *rhema*. My faith was strong because I knew God would do what He said He would do.

Dr. Paul Yonggi Cho, pastor of the largest church in Korea, tells of a great revival that broke out in his country. In the excitement of God's moving, a group of young students got a little carried away and started acting beyond their faith. They said, "Well, we can do whatever the Bible says."

One day as these young men and women were crossing the countryside, they came to a river swollen with rain. It was swift and dangerous. The students said, "The Bible says Peter walked on the water, and if Peter walked on the water, so can we." Two of them decided to try it, and they drowned! Why? Because they acted beyond their faith. Because they acted on the *logos* without the *rhema*. Jesus called Peter to walk to Him on the water, not these young people.

I'm not saying you shouldn't obey the Bible, because you should. You're to exercise your faith and cause it to grow. And if God gives you a *rhema* concerning something beyond your faith, faith will come and you will be able to stand.

Elijah acted on the Word of God

Elijah understood this. He didn't just decide one day, "Well, I'm a man of faith, and I'm tired of rain, so I'm going to stand out here and stop the rain. It's a slow day, and I don't have much to do. I haven't seen many miracles lately, so I'll just call on God to shut up the heavens."

No, when Elijah prayed, he was functioning in the *logos*, the Word of God, and I believe God quickened it to his heart. One day Elijah was reading the covenant between God and Israel in Deuteronomy 11:13-17 and the Lord quickened it to him.

This passage says, *If you faithfully obey the commands I am giving you today—to love the Lord your God and to serve him with all your heart and with all your soul—then I will send rain on your land in its season, both autumn and spring rains, so that you may gather in your grain, new wine and oil. I will provide grass in the fields for your cattle, and you will eat and be satisfied.*

Be careful, or you will be enticed to turn away and worship other gods and bow down to them. Then the Lord's anger will burn against you, and he will shut the heavens so that it will not rain and the ground will yield no produce, and you will soon perish from the good land the Lord is giving you (NIV).

Elijah read what God had promised. So when he prayed that God would shut up the heavens, he was praying in the knowledge of God's Word.

Elijah knew the Word of God, and he knew the people had turned after Baal and away from God, bowing down to idols. He read where God said He wouldn't send the rain if the people turned to false gods.

So he prayed, "God, You said that if Your people worshipped false gods, You would stop the heavens and it wouldn't rain." Elijah held God's Word up to Him and prayed earnestly for God to keep His Word, and He did.

A person of faith knows the Bible. He knows what the Bible says. When you're going through a trial, find what God says in the Bible and hold it up to Him. Remind Him of what He said. You say, "Well, if God says He's going to do it, why doesn't He just do it? Why do I have to remind Him?"

Because prayer is the power that moves the hands of God. When you stand on God's Word and remind God of His promise, it makes your faith grow. It strengthens your trust in God.

For example, God isn't automatically going to save your children. Deuteronomy 28:41 says one of the penalties for sinning is that you'll have children but not enjoy them. Now, as a Christian, Christ has redeemed you from the curse of the law (see Galatians 3:13). You can stand before God and say, "God, You said if I served You, I would enjoy my children. I believe You are going to fulfill Your promise because You never lie." And God will begin to act in your behalf to bring that promise to pass.

God isn't automatically going to fill your bank account with money. The curse of the law is to want all things but to be poor and to drag through life. But God's blessing is that you will be the head and not the tail, you will lend and not borrow, you will be on top and never on the bottom (see Deuteronomy 28:12,13).

But you must know what the Word says, take it to God, stand on faith, and He will cause it to come to pass.

Elijah had a showdown on the mountain

Elijah had to take that promise to God. God clearly stated that He would stop the rain, so why didn't He do it before? He was waiting for someone who would read the covenant, act on it, stand on it, and believe Him to bring the results.

And that's what happened. For three years and six months it didn't rain. Then, Elijah had a showdown with the prophets of Baal before the children of Israel on Mount Carmel (see 1 Kings 18:23,24).

He told the people, *Get two bulls for us. Let them* [the prophets of Baal] *choose one for themselves, and let them cut it into pieces and put it on the wood but not set fire to it. I will prepare the other bull and put it on the wood but not set fire to it. Then you call on the name of your god, and I will call on the name of the Lord. The god who answers by fire—he is God* (NIV).

The prophets of Baal spent all day trying to call down fire. They cut themselves and went through all their ceremonial rigamarole. Elijah stood over to the side and taunted them.

“Shout louder,” he told them. “Maybe your god is asleep or on a trip.” Finally, the prophets gave up.

Then Elijah gathered the people around. He repaired the altar of the Lord with twelve stones and dug a trench around it. He arranged the wood, cut the bull into pieces, and laid it on the wood. Then he told the people to fill four large jars with water and pour it on the altar. Three times, the people filled the water jugs and poured them on the offering. Elijah wanted to be sure nobody thought there was any trickery involved.

Then Elijah prayed, *O Lord, God of Abraham, Isaac and Israel, let it be known today that you are God in Israel and that I am your servant and have done all these things at your command. Answer me, O Lord, answer me, so these people will know that you, O Lord, are God, and that you are turning their hearts back again* (1 Kings 18:36,37, NIV) . And fire fell from heaven. It burned up the sacrifice, the wood, and even the stones, the soil, and the water in the trench around the altar.

The people fell down and cried, "The Lord—he is God!" Elijah commanded them to seize the prophets of Baal and kill them. Then he went off by himself to pray for rain.

The people had repented and turned back to God. Now they were in a position to receive rain, but the rain didn't automatically come. Elijah had to earnestly pray for rain. He had to stand on faith and believe that God would honor His Word.

That is what you have to do to get your needs met. Even though God has promised it and you see that it belongs to you, you're going to have to earnestly claim it. You're going to have to believe God will do what He said and stand in faith until He does.

You can't just sit around and say, "Well, God said He would do it, and I'm going to just let Him do it." No, life is a fight. Paul said to fight the good fight of faith (see 1 Timothy

6:12). You've got to claim your victory.

You've got to say "No, devil, you can't have my finances. No, you can't do this to my family." You've got to rise up and earnestly pray, even though God has already said it. There has to be some effort on your part. You've got to exercise your faith and believe God for the answer.

That's what Elijah did. He was a man of faith, and in 1 Kings 18:41-45 (NIV), he demonstrates seven qualities of faith.

1. Faith hears and sees what the world cannot hear and see

A man or woman of faith will see and hear what the world cannot see and hear.

After the prophets of Baal had been killed, Elijah found King Ahab and told him, *Go, eat and drink, for there is the sound of a heavy rain* (vs. 41). There wasn't any sign of rain in the sky, but Elijah knew God would keep His

Word. God had said, "If you break my law and worship idols, I'll keep the rain from you." Elijah had taken that word and prayed, and God had shut up the heavens.

Then Elijah had seen the people repent, and he knew he could call for the rain to come. His spirit began to reach out. He knew what God was going to do. He said, "I don't see the rain. I don't smell it or hear it, but I tell you, in my spirit, I hear the sound of abundance of rain."

A dog whistle reminds me of how faith works. If you blow a dog whistle, you won't hear a single thing. But if there's a dog nearby, his ears will perk up. He can hear that whistle. Why? Because he hears on a different sound frequency than you do.

In the same manner, Holy Ghost people can hear on a different frequency than the world. We can hear things the world does not hear. We can hear the sound of angels' wings, the sound of the footsteps of Jesus, the coming blessings of God.

Men and women of faith hear the shout of victory before it ever gets there. They can hear the sound of that wayward son or daughter coming home. By faith, they can hear the knocking on the door. They can hear the testimony of that loved one they've been praying for.

If you have faith, you hear the sound of victory before it ever gets into earshot. You hear it with the ears of faith. Why did Elijah hear the rain? Because he knew the Word of God.

2. Faith prays earnestly even though it has already heard the answer

Hearing the answer you need by faith doesn't mean you don't have to pray, to confess, to claim your victory. It doesn't mean there isn't a battle to go through. The Bible says Ahab went off to eat and drink, *but Elijah climbed to the top of Carmel, bent down to the ground and put his face between his knees* (vs. 42).

Elijah told Ahab he heard the sound of abundance of rain. So why didn't he just put his mantle over his head and walk on home. He could have said, "I heard the rain, it's coming. There's no need for me to stay around here." No, Elijah knew it was time to go before God in earnest prayer to be sure that what he had heard by faith would come to pass.

3. Faith is strong when there is no evidence of the answer

Verses 43,44 say, *"Go and look toward the sea," he told his servant. And he went up and looked.*

"There is nothing there," he said.

Men and women of faith keep going even when they don't see the answer coming. They go on when everybody is saying, "There's nothing to this act of faith. There's nothing to this healing...to this faith business. There's nothing to it."

When the doctor examines you and says, "I see nothing that tells me you're healed," you go on. When the banker says, "I see nothing that tells me you're prosperous," you go on. When the situation says, "There's no evidence that God is going to answer," you go on because you have the Word of God.

Elijah kept believing when he saw nothing. That's what God started with in the beginning. He made the universe out of nothing. So if you want to be God-like, start with nothing and speak the Word of God until what you desire comes into being.

Maybe you have nothing. You've just about given up. You've prayed and fasted. You've looked to God, and there's still nothing to show for it. The world is telling you, "It's not working!" Stand your ground. Keep holding the Word of God up to Him. In Jeremiah 1:12 the Lord says, *I am watching to see that my word is fulfilled* (NIV). If God promised it, He will do it.

4. Faith always says, "Go again!"

When you look and nothing is happening, the man or woman of faith says, "Go again. Keep going back. Don't give up."

Elijah sent his servant to look toward the sea for rain clouds. He came back and told Elijah he couldn't see any. Elijah told him to go look again. Verse 43 says, *Seven times Elijah said, "Go back."*

I imagine that servant got pretty tired. He climbed up on the hill and looked out toward the sea. He gazed and gazed. Then he went back and told Elijah, "There's nothing there."

Elijah said, "Go look again."

So the servant went a second time and looked. He came back and said, "There's still nothing there."

Elijah told him, "Go look again."

He went the third time, the fourth time, the fifth time, the sixth time. Every time his answer to Elijah was the same, "There's nothing there." Each time Elijah prayed a little bit more, then told him, "Go look again."

Elijah kept on praying. He kept on believing. He had seen God's promise in the Word. He had already heard the sound of rain. He knew if God said it, He would do it. So he just kept sending his servant to look again.

When you get discouraged and it looks like God isn't sending the answer, go again to the Word of God. Read it again. Remind God again of His promise. Go two times...three times...four times—however many times it takes—until the answer comes.

5. Faith goes on when there's just a little evidence

Verse 44 says, *The seventh time the servant reported, "A cloud as small as a man's hand is rising from the sea."* The seventh time the servant looked out over the sea, he saw a tiny cloud, not very promising, but he ran back to tell Elijah.

The man or woman of faith continues to believe and claim the victory when there is just a little evidence. The whole answer hasn't come yet. The need hasn't been completely met. But he or she keeps on believing.

You say, "I'm believing for my healing. I've been hurting all over, and I have a little relief down there in my right ankle. But it's so little." Or, "I'm believing for a financial need. I did get one bill paid, but I've got a hundred others. It's so little."

Faith goes on when there's just a little

cloud in the sky—not a big thunderhead, but a little white cloud no bigger than a man's hand.

There were many times when my wife Dodie, was fighting her battle with cancer that she saw nothing. In 1981, she was diagnosed as having metastatic cancer of the liver with only a few weeks to live. The doctors said there was nothing they could do. But she knew what God has promised in His Word. She held it up to Him and reminded Him that by His stripes she was healed (see 1 Peter 2:24). She continued to pray and believe for her complete healing even when her body was in pain and there was no evidence she would be healed.

There were many times when she had to say, "Go again. Go again. Look once more." And then she got a little relief—just a little. So she made a list of all the symptoms she was believing would leave her body. She kept confessing the Word of God in the face of symptoms and began to check them off, one by one. She saw little at first, but she went on. And today, she is completely healed.

If you see nothing, if you see just a little, go on. Hang in there. Pray earnestly. Put God in remembrance. Don't give up, and don't let the devil steal what is yours.

6. Faith believes for the big when it sees the little

Elijah said, "*Go and tell Ahab, 'Hitch up your chariot and go down before the rain stops you* '" (vs. 44). The cloud out over the sea may have been little, but Elijah knew it was the beginning of a rainstorm. He saw the little but he believed for the big. He sent word to Ahab, "That little cloud out there is the size of a man's hand, but I'm telling you, it's a sign that God's moving. You'd better hurry to get out of the rain."

Your first sign of relief may seem so small, but keep saying what God says about your situation. At the first sign of victory don't stop, back up, or retreat. That's a sign the battle has turned and the devil's on the run. That's the time to boldly proclaim you'll not be denied. You will have all that God has promised you.

7. Faith begins with nothing but ends up doing mighty things for God

Verses 45,46 say, *The sky grew black with clouds, the wind rose, a heavy rain came on and Ahab rode off to Jezreel. The power of the Lord came upon Elijah and, tucking his cloak into his belt, he ran ahead of Ahab all the way to Jezreel.*

A man or woman of faith may begin with nothing, but they'll end up with the hand of God upon them, enabling them to do mighty exploits because of what they've seen God do in the hour of their trial of faith.

Elijah never gave up. He started with nothing, and he kept praying and believing until he saw the hand-size cloud. He kept on believing until the rain came, and then, the Bible says, the hand of God came upon him, and he ran across the Valley of Jezreel. He outran the horses of Ahab! Elijah experienced the victory because he endured the test of faith. He didn't give up.

Have you been tempted to give up? I want to tell you, there are good days ahead of you. I see you running before the chariots of Ahab with the hand of God on you. I see you walking in victory in your spiritual life.

Fight on! Believe the Word of God. Don't give up because victory is just ahead of you.

BOOKS BY JOHN OSTEEN

*A Miracle For Your Marriage
*Believing God For Your Loved Ones
*Healed of Cancer *by Dodie Osteen*
*How To Claim the Benefits of the Will
*How To Demonstrate Satan's Defeat
How To Flow in the Super Supernatural
How to Release the Power of God
Overcoming Hindrances to Receiving the Baptism in the Holy Spirit
*Overcoming Opposition: How To Succeed in Doing the Will of God *by Lisa Comes*
*Pulling Down Strongholds
Reigning in Life as a King
Rivers of Living Water
*6 Lies the Devil Uses to Destroy Marriages *by Lisa Comes*
*The Believer's #1 Need
The Bible Way to Spiritual Power
The Confessions of a Baptist Preacher
*The Divine Flow
*The 6th Sense...Faith
The Truth Shall Set You Free
*There is a Miracle in Your Mouth
This Awakening Generation

(continued next page)

Unraveling the Mystery of the Blood Covenant
*What To Do When the Tempter Comes
You Can Change Your Destiny

Minibooks

*A Place Called There
*ABC's of Faith
Deception! Recognizing True and False Ministries
Four Principles in Receiving From God
How To Minister Healing to the Sick
*How to Receive Life Eternal
Keep What God Gives
*Love & Marriage
*Receive the Holy Spirit
Saturday's Coming
Seven Facts About Prevailing Prayer
Seven Qualities of a Man of Faith
*What To Do When Nothing Seems to Work

Selected titles also available in Spanish.

Please write for a complete list of prices in the Book and Tape Library of John Osteen. Write to:

Lakewood Church
P.O. Box 23297
Houston, Texas 77228